OLD TESTAMENT ARCHAEOLOGY

ALFRED HOERTH

Contents

Kregel
Publications

What Is Archaeology –
and What Can It Tell Us?

Archaeology examines the past through excavation and interpretation of the data recovered. Interpretation is the key element when it comes to utilizing the data, and widely different conclusions can result depending on whether the interpreter considers the Bible to be the Word of God or only a human document.

Some who take the Bible to be the Word of God marshal archaeological data to 'prove' the Bible. They focus on those portions of the biblical text which have been shown to be factually true – but archaeology has also uncovered textual puzzles that would not otherwise have been recognized. Frequently overlooked is the fact that archaeology does not, and cannot, prove the Bible's *theological* truth.

Some who consider the Bible to be no more than a human document point to people or events in the Bible that are uncorroborated by archaeological evidence. For them, this archaeological silence leads to the conclusion that parts of the Bible contain historical error. But insistence on external proof is unreasonable, since only a very small proportion of what was made or written in antiquity can be expected to have survived to this day. Further, very little of what is potentially recoverable has been found, let alone published for evaluation. Nevertheless, a small group (they have been called 'minimalists') has gone so far as to argue that the Old Testament is a collection of myths, devoid of any useful historical information. Unfortunately, despite their being an embarrassment to the scholarly community, minimalist pronouncements find their way into the popular press.

Archaeology is most productive when used to improve our understanding of the Bible, rather than to prove or disprove the Bible. Despite the small percentage of evidence about the ancient world recovered thus far, much is known that increases our appreciation of many biblical episodes. Archaeology fleshes out many of the people of the Bible, so that we can better understand why they behaved and wrote as they did. We can 'see' what they saw. The following pages contain many examples of how archaeology illuminates the biblical text and thus helps convey the *context* of the theological message.

Excavating the Past

The earliest excavations in the Near East were little more than treasure hunts. Greater professionalism entered the picture only gradually, and it was not until the first half of the nineteenth century that it became possible to read Egyptian hieroglyphics, or that the world of Mesopotamia opened up, with the successful translation of cuneiform.

Tell, or *Tel*, is the most common designation for ancient sites in the Near East. For protection, many ancient peoples founded their settlements on a hill and, in Old Testament times, the same sites were sometimes occupied for centuries. Over the course of time, destruction, rebuilding projects, temporary abandonment and other events resulted in new occupation-levels (strata) being built atop previous ones. A cross-section of a tell can resemble a layer cake, and some tells have been found to contain more than twenty such living levels.

Today, no one person any longer tries to oversee an excavation. Instead, a team of directors, area supervisors and specialists (for example, architects, artists, botanists, epigraphers, geologists, palaeontologists and photographers) are assembled to control the course of excavation, as well as to record and analyse the evidences as they are found.

Archaeologists generally excavate within 5- or 10-metre (15- or 30-foot) squares. The perimeters of each square (called balks) act as walkways and help keep artefacts from one square from becoming mixed with those of an adjacent square. The stratigraphy discernible on the vertical faces of the balks helps distinguish one stratum from another. Balks are generally removed when they have served their purpose and a larger horizontal exposure is desired.

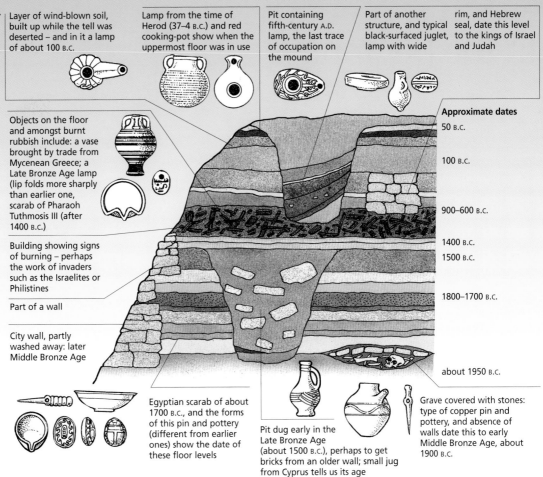

Hypothetical cross-section of a tell illustrating how a tell is formed and how distinctive pottery and other artefacts help provide dates to the individual occupation-levels.

Layer of wind-blown soil, built up while the tell was deserted – and in it a lamp of about 100 B.C.

Lamp from the time of Herod (37–4 B.C.) and red cooking-pot show when the uppermost floor was in use

Pit containing fifth-century A.D. lamp, the last trace of occupation on the mound

Part of another structure, and typical black-surfaced juglet, lamp with wide rim, and Hebrew seal, date this level to the kings of Israel and Judah

Objects on the floor and amongst burnt rubbish include: a vase brought by trade from Mycenean Greece; a Late Bronze Age lamp (lip folds more sharply than earlier one, scarab of Pharaoh Tuthmosis III (after 1400 B.C.)

Building showing signs of burning – perhaps the work of invaders such as the Israelites or Philistines

Part of a wall

City wall, partly washed away: later Middle Bronze Age

Egyptian scarab of about 1700 B.C., and the forms of this pin and pottery (different from earlier ones) show the date of these floor levels

Pit dug early in the Late Bronze Age (about 1500 B.C.), perhaps to get bricks from an older wall; small jug from Cyprus tells us its age

Grave covered with stones: type of copper pin and pottery, and absence of walls date this to early Middle Bronze Age, about 1900 B.C.

Approximate dates

50 B.C.

100 B.C.

900–600 B.C.

1400 B.C.
1500 B.C.

1800–1700 B.C.

about 1950 B.C.

In most countries of the Near East, local people are hired to do much of the manual labour, but in Israel hundreds of volunteers from around the world are attracted each year to give of their time and money to join an excavation.

When a tell contains a number of occupation-levels it is necessary carefully to distinguish each level, and keep all the architecture and artefacts belonging to it separate. This is done by paying close attention to stratigraphy and undertaking a great deal of careful recording. In this way the distinctives of each level – or stratum – can be recognized.

Objects found near the top of a tell are usually later in date than those found in a lower level. (Exceptions occur when, for example, an ancient pit has been dug into earlier levels.) But the vertical 'findspots' of objects provide only an earlier/later relationship, a relative chronology.

Early in the twentieth century it

was realized that the broken pieces of pottery (called potsherds or potshards) which litter most sites could be used to establish an absolute chronology. Ancient pottery styles changed relatively quickly, and some of that pottery is distinctive in shape and/or decoration. When pottery carrying these identifiable features was found in conjunction with, for example, a dateable inscription, that pottery could be dated to the time of the inscription. Enough such associations have been made over the decades for pottery chronology to have now become the primary tool used by archaeologists to date levels of occupation.

The Old Testament fits within what archaeologists today call the Bronze and Iron Age periods. More specifically, the kings of Israel and Judah are said to have reigned during the Iron IIB and C periods.

Today excavation techniques have

advanced far beyond the pick, shovel and basket days. Now computers and laser beam transits are viewed as essential tools. Satellite imagery is also used to locate both ancient sites and the road networks that once connected them.

The variety of evidences that can be gleaned from an excavation has also greatly increased. A geologist can determine whether excavated materials are local in origin, or evidence of trade relations. From seeds, charred wood and animal bones, botanists and palaeontologists can create a profile of the flora and fauna that existed during a specific period of time.

But, despite the present advances in archaeological knowledge and technique, one scholar estimates that only about 2 per cent of the known sites in the Near East have been sufficiently excavated. Clearly, there remains much to do and to learn.

In the Beginning

Archaeology cannot address questions concerning the antiquity of the earth and humankind – other disciplines must answer such questions. But archaeology can comment on some portions of the early chapters of Genesis.

Creation Stories

No archaeologist can excavate evidences of the creation, but extrabiblical texts can show what other cultures were saying about it during Old Testament times. We find that the Egyptians never went into any great detail about creation. One Egyptian text speaks of the god Ptah creating all the other gods. In another text, Atum is credited with this same accomplishment. And then, in a hymn to the god Amon-Re, he is called 'The Lord of truth and father of the gods' (*ANET* 365). When the Egyptians did deal with creation, their main concern was to use it to promote the primacy of this or that deity or place.

More can be found in Mesopotamian texts. There the *Enuma Elish* ('When on High') relates that the world was created as the result of a cosmic war, and people were created so that the gods would no longer have to toil. One line of the text reads: 'Out of [Kingu's] blood they fashioned mankind. Ea imposed the service and let free the gods' (*ANET* 68). Up to that time the gods had to cook their own meals, and sweep out their own temples!

This Mesopotamian creation text fills seven cuneiform tablets, only one of which is shown here. Like the stories from Egypt, it was used for political ends; in this case, to promote a city to rule. By contrast, there is no political agenda in the Genesis account. Furthermore, when compared with these other texts, Genesis is overflowing in detail.

Longevity

In the list of generations in Genesis chapter 5, the normal lifespan is much longer than the seventy years of Psalm 90:10. The Sumerian king list pictured here might help understand this. The king list records the names and lengths of reign for both pre-flood and post-flood rulers. Of the ten 'great men' who are said to have ruled before the flood, their reigns lasted from 43,200 years for Enmenlu-Anna, down to a *mere* 18,600 years for Ubar-Tutu. But for the post-flood rulers, the time spans are greatly reduced. Perhaps the king list reflects a memory of longer lifespans in the distant past.

The Flood

Genesis chapters 6–9 tell of a flood which only eight people in the world survived. Several decades ago it was reported that evidence of the flood had been found – a 2.5-metre- (8-foot-) thick flood deposit – during excavation of Ur, in southern Mesopotamia. However, it was subsequently revealed that two silt deposits were involved, not one as originally reported, and that a brief re-occupation separated the two. Then, other excavations no more than 24 kilometers (15 miles) away found no comparable 'flood layer'. Unfortunately, the initial announcement received such extensive press coverage that echoes of it still persist.

Repeated attempts have been made by 'arkeologists' to find Noah's ark. No claims of its discovery have been backed by convincing evidence, and more than one has been a hoax. Genesis 8:4 says that 'the ark came to rest on the mountains of Ararat'. Ararat – Urartu in Mesopotamian texts – covers a large and mountainous area in eastern Turkey. Ancient traditions put the landing place for the ark in several different locations, and the extinct volcano presently favoured was not even a candidate prior to the eleventh or twelfth centuries A.D.

Flood Stories outside the Bible

Before Abraham was born in Mesopotamia, the Sumerians had composed a story in which a man named Ziusudra escaped a flood by means of a boat. 'The flood had swept over the land, and the huge boat had been tossed about by the windstorms on the great waters' (*ANET* 44). When danger passed, Ziusudra opened a window in the boat and made a sacrifice to the gods. This Sumerian flood story was later incorporated into the Gilgamesh Epic, which became so popular that copies of it have been found outside

One of the seven clay tablets containing the *Enuma Elish*, the Mesopotamian story of creation.

This clay prism, dating from approximately 2000 B.C., is one of more than a dozen known copies of the Sumerian king list.

Tablet 11 of the Assyrian version of the Gilgamesh Epic. The epic is recorded on twelve tablets; this one contains Utnapishtim's account of the flood.

Mesopotamia. In the epic, the man who built a boat and escaped the flood was called Utnapishtim. 'The weather was awesome to behold. I boarded the ship and battened up the entrance. . . . For one day the south storm blew, gathering speed as it blew, submerging the mountains, overtaking the people like a battle' (*ANET* 94). In time, his boat came to rest on a mountain.

Utnapishtim sent out first a dove and then a swallow, but they returned to the boat. Then he sent out a raven. 'The raven went forth and, seeing that the water had diminished, he eats, circles, caws, and turns not round' (*ANET* 95). Utnapishtim then left the boat and made a sacrifice.

The Gilgamesh Epic provides a good example of how interpretation shapes conclusions. For those who do not believe the Bible to be an inspired document, the similarities in the accounts, and the fact that the epic was written earlier than the book of Genesis, is evidence that the Genesis account is no more than a myth adapted from the earlier work.

Some who believe the Bible is the Word of God respond by emphasizing the dissimilarities between the epic and Genesis in order to play down any meaningful connection between the two works. Yet for others, similarities are simply due to both accounts going back to a common source, the event. For them, dissimilarities are to be expected when details are recast to fit a polytheistic world view. Nor is it surprising that some details, including the use of birds, are in both versions, because this is what actually happened.

Tower of Babel

In some modern artistic renderings, the tower mentioned in Genesis 11 resembles a Mesopotamian ziggurat (for a ziggurat, see pages 23, 28). Temple towers did not develop into ziggurats until near the end of the third millennium, after the appearance of cuneiform and hieroglyphic writing. Therefore, the statement in Genesis 11:1 that construction began when 'the whole world had one language and a common speech', makes these depictions highly unlikely.

Everywhere else in the Old Testament, the Hebrew word *migdal*, translated 'tower' in Genesis 11:4–5, refers to a tower or fortress into which defenders of a city could retreat as a last line of defence. It would seem more probable that this, rather than a ziggurat, is what the citizens were beginning to construct.

The Patriarchs

Ebla

In 1974 thousands of clay tablets were found at the ancient site of Ebla. Initial reports claimed that such close parallels had been found, for instance with the cities mentioned in Genesis chapter 14, that patriarchal history would have to be rewritten. The alleged parallels have since been found to be erroneous. Ebla remains an important discovery for early Near-Eastern – but not biblical – history.

Abraham in Mesopotamia

Abraham spent the first part of his life in Ur, in southern Mesopotamia. The Bible skims over those years, but archaeology has uncovered much about the society that surrounded him. The city of Ur covered some 62 hectares (150 acres), and houses were generally two-storied and built around a central courtyard. Their thick mud-brick walls provided insulation against harsh summer temperatures. On the whole, housing was quite comfortable, and not very different from houses today in rural areas of Iraq.

From statues and texts we learn that most men – presumably including Abraham – wore a moustache and full beard. Women in Sarah's day were very interested in jewellery and hairstyles. Clothing in Mesopotamia was somewhat similar to that worn millennia later by the Romans.

Collections of laws disclose the relative worth of different occupations, and the relative cost of certain commodities. Moneylenders were charging interest of between 20 and 33.3 per cent and, when a debt was in default, it was legal to enslave someone from the debtor's house until payment was made.

Marriage laws provide much detail concerning the procedures involved in getting married and staying wed. From these we learn that it was accepted for a man to divorce a barren wife. Thus we recognize how deeply Abraham loved Sarah; though she was barren, he did not divorce her.

Religion was a large part of every Mesopotamian's life. The Bible says Abraham's father, Terah, was a polytheist (Joshua 24:2). He would have worshipped the moon god, the chief deity of Ur. He would also have accepted that thousands of other gods existed, and that it was his duty to serve them. Service consisted of participating in certain temple ceremonies and duties. It also meant feeding, washing, and clothing the private deity statue kept in the home. Mesopotamians believed in both black and white magic, that the gods might not always act reasonably, demons could cause harm, and that neighbours might engage in witchcraft.

The Bible does not indicate whether initially Abraham embraced his father's religion. If he did, it was a giant step of faith when he began to worship the true God.

Terah took his extended family, which included Abraham and Sarah, several hundred miles north-west to Haran (Genesis 11:31). No reason is given for the move, but ancient texts reveal that the agricultural base was deteriorating in southern Mesopotamia, and the political scene had become chaotic due to repeated infighting among cities.

As in Ur, the chief deity of Haran was the moon god, which could explain why Terah stopped there.

Beni Hasan tomb painting depicting people entering Egypt from Canaan. This Egyptian painting dates very close to the time of Abraham and Sarah, and provides another window into patriarchal life, showing changes the two would have been expected to make in adapting to life in Canaan. The men wear kilts or long garments fitted over one shoulder. The over-the-shoulder garments of the women are longer, but similarly multicoloured. The men wear sandals, while the women's footwear resembles a slipper-sock. The women wear head-bands and have long hair. Unlike in Mesopotamia, the men have trimmed beards, but no moustaches. The painting also depicts weaponry. One man appears to carry a water-skin, one plays a lyre, and two objects are tentatively identified as bellows.

Camels

The scattered mentions of camels in the patriarchal stories are still occasionally pointed to as an obvious error in the Bible – with the argument that camels were not domesticated until much later. But sufficient data has accumulated to show that camels were indeed used early in the second millennium B.C.

The Story of Sinuhe

Prior to Abraham's entry into Canaan, an Egyptian named Sinuhe took up residence there. Exodus 3:8 describes a 'land flowing with milk and honey'. In the Egyptian text about Sinuhe we read:

> It was a good land . . . Figs were in it, and grapes. It had more wine than water. Plentiful was its honey, abundant its olives. Every kind of fruit was on its trees. Barley was there, and emmer. There was no limit to any kind of cattle. . . . Bread was made for me as daily fare, wine as daily provision, cooked meat and roast fowl, beside the wild beasts of the desert, for they hunted for me and laid before me, beside the catch of my own hounds. (*ANET* 19–20)

A collection of inscribed weights; the arrow points to a weight marked 2 shekels. Such weights make it possible to translate ancient terms into modern ones. For instance, the 400 shekels of silver Abraham used to purchase a burial site for Sarah (Genesis 23:16) would weigh, in today's terms, about 4.5 kilograms (10 pounds).

The story goes on to relate much more about Palestine, mirroring and amplifying the picture given in the Bible. Sinuhe lets us see the patriarchal world through other eyes.

The Patriarchs in Palestine

Archaeology has similarly recovered much of the fabric of Canaanite life. It was a time of potential wealth, but the excavated destruction levels of

The city gateway at Dan as excavated (left) and in an artist's restoration (below). This gateway is typical of the patriarchal period; two sets of piers stand behind the outside entrance. An enemy would have to break through three separate gates to gain entry.

tells show it could also be a time of danger. Not surprisingly, much attention was paid to strong city walls and gateways. More than just a necessary break in a defensive wall allowing people to enter and exit a city, the gate area was also often used as the marketplace, and somewhere travellers could sleep overnight. Lot and the gateway at Sodom come to mind in this context (Genesis 19:1). Gateways were also the legal centre of a city, and it was to the gateway that Abraham went to purchase a burial place for Sarah (Genesis 23:10).

Cuneiform tablets (the Nuzi texts) contain societal customs that were practised over much of the Near East. From them we learn that childless couples adopted so that the family name could continue, and so that, in time, the adopted children would give the couple a proper burial. Sarah encouraged Abraham to father a child through her handmaiden – another acceptable solution. The surrogate mother took on the rank of 'other wife', and the bride might be obligated in a prenuptial document to provide for that other woman, should she prove barren. Further, should a child be born, the wife was not to try, as Sarah did, to drive away the other woman and her child.

The birthright and the role of the eldest son are prominent in both the Nuzi texts and the patriarchal stories. Wealth and power usually transferred to the eldest son. In one Nuzi text, Hupitaya's inheritance was divided so that his eldest son received a double share. According to the texts, the birthright might be voluntarily forfeited (compare the story of Jacob and Esau's birthright, Genesis 25:27–34).

Joseph and Moses in Egypt

By the time Abraham visited Egypt, the famous pyramids at Giza were already several hundred years old. And by the time of Joseph, the Egyptians were no longer constructing any pyramids.

Joseph

Joseph was sold into an Egypt different politically from the Egypt Abraham had known. People called 'Hyksos' by the Egyptians had entered the Nile delta from Canaan and taken control of lower (northern) Egypt. Culturally, however, Egypt would have seemed little changed; the Hyksos had adopted much of the Egyptian way of life. For example, they wrote in hieroglyphics, used Egyptian titles and worshipped the Egyptian god Seth.

Joseph was sold into slavery, but rose to a responsible position before being thrown into jail on a false charge of attempted rape. Dreams were then thought to be a way by which the gods informed people what they should do, or what was going to happen. After Joseph had demonstrated his ability to 'read' dreams, he warned Pharaoh of impending famine. Egyptian agriculture was very dependent on the Nile, which yearly brought both water and needed nourishment into the fields. But, despite an early-warning system far up river (either too little or too much flooding could be devastating), the Egyptians lived with memories of years of famine and with the possibility that it could happen again. In this light, it is not surprising that, after his important warning, Joseph was raised from prison to a high governmental position.

Genesis 41:42–43 records Joseph's elevation to power, and contains several distinctive Egyptian touches: the 'signet ring' (scarab ring), the 'robes of fine linen', the 'gold chain', the 'chariot' (chariots were introduced into Egypt by the Hyksos) and the call to 'bow down' (a form of respect seen in Egyptian paintings).

In time both Jacob and then Joseph died and were mummified. There are no secret arts of embalming. The most important steps in the mummification process were the dehydration of the body and protection against future moisture and infestation.

Genesis 50:26 says Joseph 'died at the age of a hundred and ten'. This, however, is not necessarily his exact age at death. In Egypt the number 110 was used when wishing someone a long life, or when indicating that someone had lived to a ripe old age.

Moses

By the time Moses was born, the Hyksos had been forcibly thrown out, and Egypt's New Kingdom had begun. The oppression recorded in the Bible was primarily a reaction to the Hyksos takeover, and fear that, should there be too many Hebrews, foreign domination could reoccur.

This illustration is based on an excavated Egyptian estate, and provides an idea of the type of setting in which Joseph functioned as an overseer for Potiphar. (Roofs have been omitted to show interior construction.) The main building has vents near the first-floor ceiling so that hot air can escape the rooms, but large windows are provided upstairs. Silos (in the foreground) have staircases so that the newest grain could be poured into the top, and the oldest grain extracted through lower doors. Storerooms, workrooms and servant quarters are adjacent to the main building.

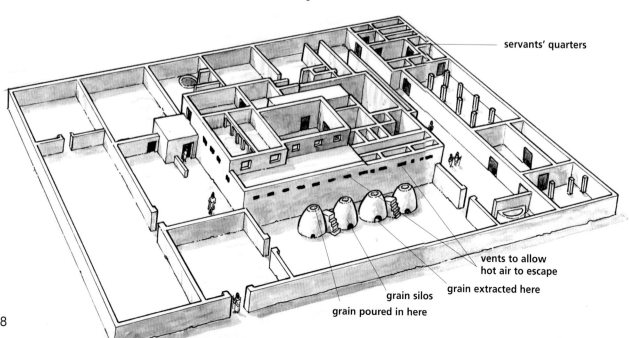

servants' quarters

vents to allow hot air to escape

grain extracted here

grain silos

grain poured in here

This tomb-painting depicts various stages of brick-making, from mixing water and mud, to forming the mixture in moulds and setting the bricks out to dry. Finally, the bricks were gathered for use. Straw was usually added as a binder to keep the bricks from breaking as they dried. An Egyptian text from later in the New Kingdom states that fifty bricks per worker was the daily quota.

Early in the New Kingdom, Egyptian armies repeatedly campaigned in and beyond Canaan. Most campaigns were little more than parades of strength, and crown princes from various cities in Canaan were brought back to Egypt as hostages to ensure the continuing loyalty of their fathers. It was also hoped that the princes would become pro-Egyptian and, thus, useful later when allowed to return home. Acts 7:22 states that 'Moses was educated in all the wisdom of the Egyptians'. He was perhaps an early recipient of this acculturation policy.

Moses was forced to flee Egypt for a number of years but when the pharaoh who had oppressed the Hebrews died (Exodus 2:23) God called Moses back to lead his people from Egypt into the Promised Land. Pharaohs of the early eighteenth dynasty have been characterized as extroverts and 'sportsmen kings'. Egyptian texts laud their athletic ability and other prowess. In one text Amenhotep II drew 300 bows to test their quality and then, from a moving chariot, shot arrows through copper targets nearly 7 centimetres (3 inches) thick, 'a deed which had never been done nor heard of' (ANET 244). Such hyperbolic accounts make it easy to understand both Moses' reluctance to confront Pharaoh, and the king's response to him.

Why the Egyptian Silence?

So far, nothing has been found in the Egyptian records that can be directly linked to Joseph, Moses or any part of the Hebrews' sojourn in Egypt. There are two separate explanations for this silence:
1. After the expulsion of the Hyksos, the Egyptians made a concerted effort to wipe that time of occupation from memory. This was so successful that today it is not even possible to compile a complete list of Hyksos pharaohs, let alone their subordinates. It is likely that any Egyptian record that might have existed concerning Joseph has been lost in that purge of history.
2. Egyptians seldom recorded setbacks. No records would have been made of the series of plagues or of the successful flight of the Hebrews.

The Bible does not name the pharaohs who ruled during the time of Moses. Egyptologists have established that initially the title 'pharaoh' stood alone in Egyptian texts. It was not until the tenth century B.C. that the title began to be followed by the name of the specific king. The biblical writers were simply following Egyptian precedent.

A strict reading of what little biblical chronology there is for the second millennium B.C. points to Thutmose III as the pharaoh who caused the Hebrews so much suffering, and to Amenhotep II as the pharaoh of the Exodus. In the mid-twentieth century, however, archaeological evidences were used to link Rameses II with the Exodus, and what is known about his flamboyant years as pharaoh would certainly fit the identification. This identification, however, requires a less than literal reading of certain biblical verses, and in recent years the archaeological evidences used in support of Rameses II as the pharaoh of the Exodus have been found erroneous.

The Exodus and Years in Sinai

The Exodus from Egypt

The Exodus began from Egypt's eastern delta. Of the places mentioned in that area, Rameses has been identified with Tell ed-Daba. Two sites have long vied as the possible location of Pithom. Recent limited excavation has ruled one out, and has shown the other, Tell er-Retaba, still to be a viable candidate. But, aside from showing where to place dots on a biblical map, archaeology has added little to our knowledge of the route taken out of Egypt.

Exodus 13:17 tells us the north-easterly routes directly into Canaan were ruled out because the Hebrews would then 'face war'. From both excavation and Egyptian texts, it is known that a string of forts (only one is indicated on the map) called by the Egyptians the 'Walls of the Ruler', ran along the northern border. Current excavation is adding to our knowledge of these forts, but it is already clear that no large group of fugitives could have evaded them, but would definitely 'face war' if they tried to pass.

Moses led his people across the Red Sea (Reed Sea in Hebrew) and into the Sinai peninsula. Various crossing-points have been suggested but they are all tentative.

One archaeologist has attempted to identify Mt. Sinai with a hill in northern Sinai, but the Bible makes it clear that the Hebrews turned south. The recent claim that Mt. Sinai has been found in Saudi Arabia has no archaeological support. The traditional identification of Mt. Sinai is with Jebel Musa, the 'mountain of Moses' in Arabic. There are other, and taller, heights in this mountainous southern area, but the early church accepted Jebel Musa as the correct spot. St. Catherine's Monastery was built at its foot in the sixth century.

Biblical Law and Ancient Near-Eastern Law

At Mt. Sinai God stressed to his people through Moses that there were specific ways in which they were to be different. For instance, they had just come out of Egypt, where gods were fashioned in both human and animal form. They would enter Canaan, where idols were cast in human form. The second commandment forbids such practices.

Biblical law is often compared with the Code of Hammurapi, a collection of laws which was compiled almost three hundred years before Moses stopped at Mt. Sinai. A few obvious similarities have long been recognized:

> If men who are fighting hit a pregnant woman and she gives birth prematurely . . . the offender must be fined whatever the woman's husband demands.
> (Exodus 21:22)

> If a man struck another man's daughter and has caused her to have a miscarriage, he shall pay ten shekels of silver for her foetus.
> (Code of Hammurapi 209: *ANET* 175)

Such similarities are to be expected, and they are evidence of a 'common' law which then operated in the Near East. But in other ways biblical law was unique.

Should Old Testament punishment be thought harsh, it needs to be recognized that it was equally harsh for everyone. The Code of Hammurapi law quoted above dealt with two aristocrats. In law 211, if an aristocrat 'caused a commoner's

This nearly 2.5-metre- (8-foot-) tall diorite stele is known as the Code of Hammurapi. Approximately three hundred laws were written in cuneiform on its sides. The bottom portion of the stele was defaced in ancient times, but what remains clearly shows it to be a selection of laws; it does not pretend to be comprehensive. Correctly speaking, then, it is not a 'code'. At the top of the stele, Hammurapi, king of Babylon, faces the seated figure of the god Marduk.

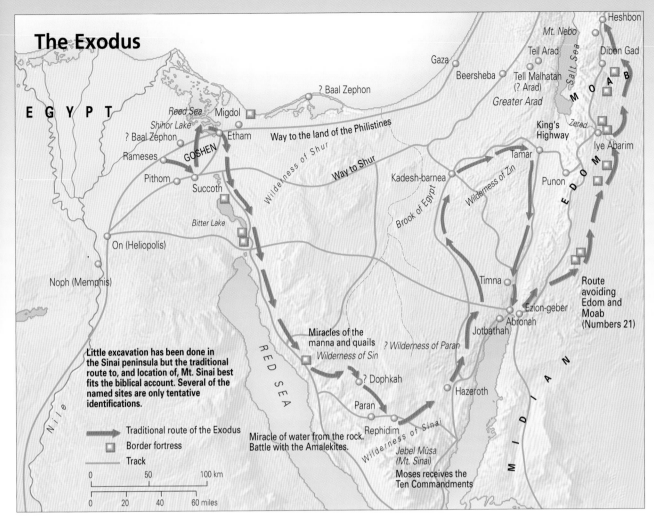

The Exodus

EGYPT

Heshbon
Mt. Nebo
Tell Arad
Dibon Gad
Gaza
Beersheba
Tell Malhatah (? Arad)
Greater Arad
MOAB
? Baal Zephon
Reed Sea   Migdol
Shihor Lake
? Baal Zephon   Etham   Way to the land of the Philistines
Rameses   GOSHEN
Way to Shur
Wilderness of Shur
King's Highway
Zered
Pithom
Succoth
Tamar
IYE Abarim
Kadesh-barnea
Brook of Egypt
Wilderness of Zin
Punon
EDOM
Bitter Lake
On (Heliopolis)
Noph (Memphis)
Timna
Route avoiding Edom and Moab (Numbers 21)
Miracles of the manna and quails   ? Wilderness of Paran
Wilderness of Sin
Ezion-geber
Abronah
Jotbathah
Nile
Little excavation has been done in the Sinai peninsula but the traditional route to, and location of, Mt. Sinai best fits the biblical account. Several of the named sites are only tentative identifications.
RED SEA
? Dophkah
Hazeroth
MIDIAN
Paran
Rephidim   Wilderness of Sinai
Jebel Mûsa (Mt. Sinai)

Miracle of water from the rock.
Battle with the Amalekites.
Moses receives the Ten Commandments

Traditional route of the Exodus
Border fortress
Track

0   50   100 km
0   20   40   60 miles

daughter to have a miscarriage, he shall pay five shekels of silver' (*ANET* 175). In law 213, if he caused another aristocrat's slave 'to have a miscarriage, he shall pay two shekels of silver' (*ANET* 175). Ten shekels, five shekels, two shekels of silver; here the punishment did not fit the crime, rather it fitted one's status in society.

There was also gender discrimination. In the Bible, equal punishment was to be meted out to both participants. In cases of adultery both were put to death. In other societies only the woman was put to death.

A study of ancient Near-Eastern treaties finds that a complex but consistent outline was followed in the mid-second millennium B.C., and that biblical law was cast within a 'suzerain-vassal treaty' format. In the Bible, God is the suzerain/king, and the Hebrews are his vassals/people.

The study further shows that, after 1200 B.C., this elaborate format was replaced by a simpler and less rigid treaty formula. Therefore, had the books of Exodus and Deuteronomy been written late in the first millennium B.C., there is almost no possibility that its writers would have known of, let alone used, the earlier and more elaborate format. So even the language and form in which the biblical laws are cast is an argument for their being Mosaic in date. Another consequence of this study of ancient treaties is the recognition that not only the words, but even the format, spoke forcefully to the Hebrews concerning their relationship with God.

After Sinai

After staying in southern Sinai a little less than a year, Moses led the people northward. When they reached Kadesh-barnea, the Promised Land was almost in sight. The oasis Ain el-Qudeirat is generally accepted as the site of Kadesh-barnea. Thus far, there is no evidence of settlement prior to the tenth century B.C., but little of the area has been tested to virgin soil.

As in Sinuhe's story centuries earlier (page 7), an advance party found Canaan to be a rich land (Numbers 13:27), but fearsomely fortified. When a Hebrew army marched north, it was sent reeling back to Kadesh-barnea in defeat. And there the people stayed for nearly forty years, until God gave them permission to continue on. Their 'Wilderness Wandering' is best understood as a movement from one oasis to another in the vicinity of Kadesh-barnea.

The Conquest and the Judges

The Conquest

Moses led his people northwards around the east side of the Dead Sea. While the terrain would have presented serious difficulties, the Bible focuses on the military and spiritual challenges. In Numbers 22 a man was hired to curse the approaching Hebrews into defeat. Surprisingly, a memory of this episode was discovered at the site of Deir Alla, perhaps biblical Succoth, where the excavators found fragments of a text dealing with 'Balaam son of Beor', the Balaam of Numbers 22, written on a plastered wall. The text dates several centuries after the event and, not surprisingly, changes to the story had crept in;

rather than God, one line reads, 'The gods came to him at night.'

The Hebrews moved into position at the north-east end of the Dead Sea. Joshua, now in command, sent spies into Jericho, which was on the eastern access route into Canaan and had to be neutralized before the Hebrews could enter the land. After a week of what some have called psychological warfare, the walls of the city were breached and a foothold was won in the Promised Land.

After they had climbed to the central hill country, the city of Ai became the Hebrews' next target. Et Tell is generally identified as biblical Ai, but no sign of occupation or destruction has been found that can be linked with the conquest. Perhaps biblical Ai lies under the modern

Arab town which covers much of the site, but another possibility now being investigated is that a nearby tell may contain the remains of the biblical city.

The Hebrews took time at Shechem to erect an altar and make offerings to God. Then conflict resumed at Gibeon, and a series of battles flowed south-west down from the hill country. At one point five kings were captured and Joshua directed his officers to put their 'feet on the necks of these kings' (Joshua 10:24). However excessive this act might seem today, Joshua was following established custom. In the ancient Near East, this was a way to show mastery over an enemy.

The Hebrews pacified the north largely in a single attack on a coalition gathering at Hazor. Hazor is described as 'the head of all these kingdoms' (Joshua 11:10), and archaeology brings meaning to that description. From the many Near-Eastern sites excavated over the years, we know that an average city covered some 6–8 hectares (15–20 acres) – by contrast Hazor occupied 81 hectares (200 acres).

Their literature provides a glimpse into the religious beliefs and actions of the Canaanites and, therefore, into what God found so distasteful. God had long shown mercy (Genesis 15:16), but now time had run out.

The Amarna Letters

At the time of the conquest, Canaan was in economic and political turmoil. This state of affairs is reflected in the Amarna Letters, correspondence written largely between Canaanite princes and the Egyptian court. As mentioned on page 9, Egypt had begun imposing control in Canaan by taking Canaanite princes as hostages for indoctrination. Now, however, Egypt was distracted and Canaanites used to its protection were left without support. Repeatedly they begged Egypt for help, while accusing one another of disloyalty to Pharaoh.

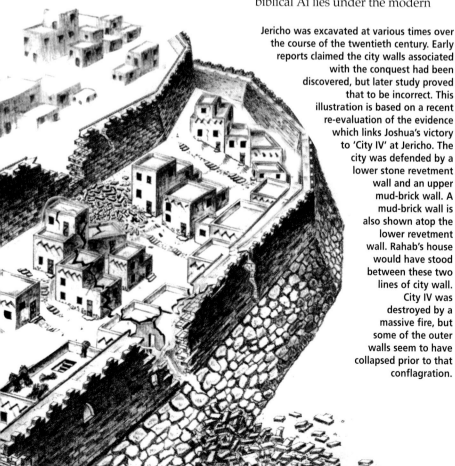

Jericho was excavated at various times over the course of the twentieth century. Early reports claimed the city walls associated with the conquest had been discovered, but later study proved that to be incorrect. This illustration is based on a recent re-evaluation of the evidence which links Joshua's victory to 'City IV' at Jericho. The city was defended by a lower stone revetment wall and an upper mud-brick wall. A mud-brick wall is also shown atop the lower revetment wall. Rahab's house would have stood between these two lines of city wall. City IV was destroyed by a massive fire, but some of the outer walls seem to have collapsed prior to that conflagration.

Under David Israel became a powerful player in Near-Eastern politics, a position he attained through a skilful combination of diplomacy and military conquest. Archaeologists have found that northern cities such as Megiddo, Taanach, Ibleam and Beth-shan have strata showing destruction or extensive changes in their city plans at about the time of David. It seems certain that these main route-centres were conquered during David's reign.

Archaeology provides little new insight into David's personal life. We are a bit clearer about Uriah, Bathsheba's husband. In 2 Samuel 11:3 he is identified as a Hittite but, more precisely, he was a Neo-Hittite. The Hittite nation collapsed about midway through the period of the judges, but some people in the provinces of the fallen empire continued aspects of Hittite culture for several more centuries. Uriah, and the Hittites with whom Solomon would deal, were part of this 'afterglow'.

Psalms

David is credited with nearly half of the 150 psalms in the book of Psalms. A good number of ancient musical instruments and depictions of people playing musical instruments have been found. The Hebrew names for musical instruments are better understood than just a few decades ago, and these evidences make it possible to visualize Old Testament worship more correctly. Canaanite musical notation and Babylonian tuning instructions have also been found, but we are not yet able to replicate the music that accompanied the psalms.

These fragments from a stele were found in 1993 and 1994 during the excavation of the northern site of Dan. They are examples of the way archaeology repeatedly has an impact upon biblical studies. Although this 'Dan Inscription' dates to the ninth century – post-David – one line contains the phrase 'house of David'. This is the first recognized extra-biblical reference to David ever found. It was discovered at a time when minimalists (see p. 2) were strenuously insisting that David (and Solomon) were fictitious characters. Although the fragments were found by one of the most respected of the Israeli archaeologists, minimalists were reduced to calling it a forgery!

This ivory box, here shown almost life size, was probably part of the treasure taken from Syro-Palestine when the Assyrians began sending their armies westward. The musicians are depicted playing string, percussion and wind instruments.

One of David's first acts as king of Israel was to capture Jerusalem from the Jebusites and make it his capital city; Hebron was too closely identified with Judah. Jerusalem, although small (only about 4 hectares [10 acres]) was better situated strategically, militarily and economically. Additionally, Jerusalem was well protected on three sides by deep valleys, needing additional protection only on the north. Of more concern was Jerusalem's fresh water supply, which came from a spring on its eastern slope. Archaeologists have found that this spring was guarded by towers, and that a tunnel fed water back into the city. David instructed his men to attack by way of the water shaft (2 Samuel 5:8). Although there is much controversy over some aspects of the tunnel, it was the means by which Jerusalem became the City of David.

Solomon

Solomon the Builder

Under Solomon Jerusalem tripled in size and building projects were also carried out throughout the country. An enigmatic reference in 1 Kings 7:12 refers to buildings constructed with 'three courses of dressed stone and one course of trimmed cedar beams'. Archaeologists have found that this was an Anatolian practice introduced into Israel by Phoenician craftsmen; the beams acted as shock absorbers during earthquakes, which were well known in Palestine and Anatolia.

The three cities mentioned with Jerusalem in 1 Kings 9:15 (Hazor, Megiddo and Gezer) were all strategically located. Hazor guarded the northern entrance into Israel, Megiddo controlled a main route within the land, and Gezer monitored the route connecting Jerusalem with the coast. Each city was also adjacent to areas of flat terrain, where Solomon's large chariot force could be effectively deployed. Solomonic city gateways have been found at all three sites. In Patriarchal times (see page 7) three sets of doors barred an enemy from entry to a city. In Solomon's day, an additional set of piers – and doors – protected the cities.

'Solomon's stables' at Megiddo have long served as an example of the way archaeology illuminates the Bible. However, archaeological research is not static, and recent excavations have uncovered similar buildings elsewhere which had clearly been used as storerooms, not stables. Their simple architectural plan made such structures easily adaptable to either purpose. Even the date of the Megiddo 'stables' has been questioned. If they are later than Solomon (see page 21), his own stables may still be awaiting excavation, deeper inside the tell.

Solomon's Temple

In his fourth year, Solomon began to construct the temple in Jerusalem. In plan it was similar to the tabernacle, except for the addition of a porch, and storage areas along three sides.

In older recreations the porch columns are shown freestanding and were assigned some very outlandish symbolism. One writer went as far as to state that the columns were evidence that Solomon slipped into paganism early in his reign. But God would not have accepted the temple (1 Kings 8:10–11) if this were so and, based on parallels in other temple and palace plans, current illustrations show the columns as load-bearing within the porch.

The temple was twice as large as the tabernacle had been, but was still only 27 metres (90 feet) long, 9 metres (30 feet) wide and 13.5 metres (45 feet) tall. Seven years were required to construct

Ground plans of the city gates at Megiddo, Hazor and Gezer. The gates at Hazor and Gezer were joined to 'casemate' walls. Casemate walls consisted of double walls joined by cross walls. To an enemy the casemate wall would appear as formidable as a solid wall, but it saved in labour and material. In peacetime the interior space could be used for storage or housing, and in time of war it would be filled in wherever the defences were threatened.

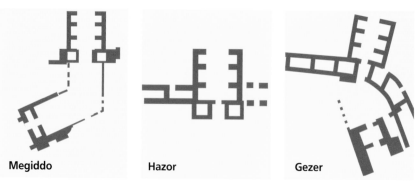

Megiddo   Hazor   Gezer

One of the 'stable' areas found at Megiddo as actually excavated, and (inset) a model showing the buildings restored, cut away to show their interior.

this modest-sized structure; in that day the importance of a place of worship was not reflected in its size.

For many years Solomon's (and Herod's) temple were believed to have stood where the Dome of the Rock now stands in Jerusalem. Then, in the 1980s, much attention was given to the argument that the temple was actually located some 91.5 meters (300 feet) to the north. Since then, new evidences have shown the original location to be correct.

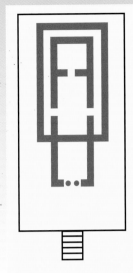

Solomon's temple

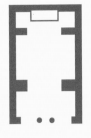

Tayinat temple, Syria

Ain Dara temple, Syria

Solomon's temple was similar in size and plan to two temples excavated in Syria. In both, the columns fronting the building are within the roofline. One temple, like Solomon's, even has storage areas around three sides. This similarity in plan should not worry the Bible student; the architecture itself is neutral.

External Contacts

In 1 Kings 3:1 Solomon married a princess from the north of Egypt. Many years earlier a king of Babylon had signed a peace treaty with Egypt. Instead of the princess he expected as part of the agreement, he received a letter explaining that Egyptian state policy did not allow a princess to be given in marriage outside the country. The Babylonian king was not pleased, but responded that he would settle for a beautiful woman whom he could pass off as a king's daughter! Solomon's marriage to the princess came at a time when Egypt was divided; one pharaoh ruled in the north and another in the south. The northern pharaoh found a formidable power on his border and thought it expedient to break a centuries-old article of foreign policy.

1 Kings 10 records the visit of the queen of Sheba to Israel. Sheba (Saba, in extra-biblical texts) was at the south-west end of the Arabian Peninsula. Assyrian records show that Arabian queens played prominent political roles in the early first millennium, and it is likely that she was sent by her husband to negotiate with Solomon. There was reason to worry that Solomon's fleet in the Red Sea would negatively impact Saba's caravan trade.

Proverbs

Proverbs were popular throughout the Near East; copying and compiling them was a court pastime. Solomon left us hundreds of proverbs, but thousands more have been found:

> Let what is mine remain unused, let me use up what is yours! – will this endear a man to the household of his friend?
> Possessions are sparrows in flight which can find no place to alight.
> Tell a lie and then tell the truth: it will be considered a lie!
> He was made to dwell near the water, but he looks toward the uplands without looking at their rigors! (Gordon, 1.8, 18, 71, 149)

Today we would say, 'The grass is always greener on the other side of the fence.'

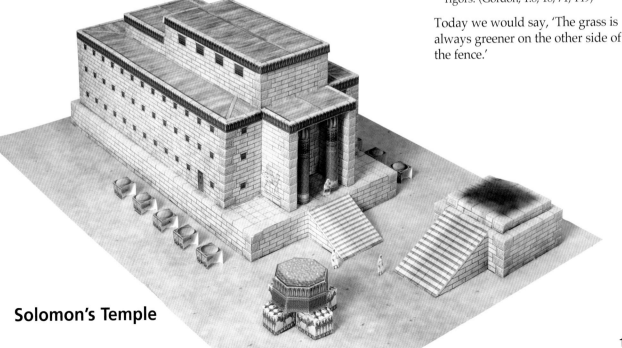

Solomon's Temple

Early Divided Kingdom 931–841 B.C.

In the Year of . . .

The biblical writers gave little attention to the passage of time until the tenth century B.C., when some events were even tied to a specific day, month and year. But this wealth of data must be understood within the complex dating systems then in use. There were two ways of counting the first year of a king's reign, and Judah and Israel began their year at different points on the calendar. Sometimes both a king and his son took full credit for their years of joint rule. This is not the place to examine these and other complexities, but only to state that seeming chronological 'errors' can be resolved.

It was also in the tenth century that both Egyptian and biblical records begin providing the specific name of the pharaohs (see page 9).

The Opening Years

When Rehoboam refused to lower taxes, he was suddenly reduced to being king of little more than Judah. Jeroboam became king of Israel, quickly closed his southern border and designated Dan and Bethel as alternate worship sites. A raised platform discovered at Dan might be the high place on which a golden calf was placed (1 Kings 12:28–29).

Five years after the death of Solomon, an Egyptian army swept into Judah. The biblical account tells of the pressure put on Jerusalem, but archaeology adds more detail. On a temple wall in Egypt, Pharaoh Shishak – the first pharaoh to be named in the Bible – listed more than 150 places he claimed that he defeated in this campaign – including sites far north in Israel. There is no hint in the Bible that his army continued northwards, and Shishak is known to have sometimes exaggerated his exploits. In this case, however, he can be trusted; a stele fragment bearing his name was found at Megiddo where he had had it erected. Pharaoh Shishak sought to reassert Egypt's control over the land but, in the event, his campaign was little more than a raid.

Pharaoh had given Solomon a princess. Why, after Solomon died, did the next pharaoh attack his son? Because it was a native Egyptian pharaoh who gave the princess to Solomon, and Pharaoh Shishak was a Libyan. In the intervening years, Egypt had been taken over by Libyans, and the Egyptian princess and the political tie meant nothing to the new pharaoh.

Later Years

The political instability that characterized the northern kingdom is reflected by the shifts in capitals – first to Shechem, then Tirzah and finally to Samaria. Although strategically placed, Samaria was not

Detail from a wall relief in the Karnak temple at Thebes, Upper Egypt, commemorating Shishak's raid into Judah and Israel. Shishak brandishes a sword in one hand and holds ropes connected to ovals (cartouches) in the other. Each oval contains the name of a place that Shishak claims to have defeated. Bound bodies are attached to each oval.

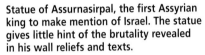

Statue of Assurnasirpal, the first Assyrian king to make mention of Israel. The statue gives little hint of the brutality revealed in his wall reliefs and texts.

The Moabite Stone. The Moabite Stone was one of the earliest archaeological finds to relate to the Bible. The stele was originally found whole, but was shattered before it reached scholarly hands. Fortunately, impressions had been made before this happened, and it was possible to recover most of the text.

Carved ivory inlay from Samaria. It is sometimes inferred from 1 Kings 22:39 that Ahab lived in a house made of ivory. In reality, the reference is to ivory panels such as this which the wealthy used to decorate their doorways and furniture.

occupied until late in Omri's reign. The lack of a good water supply had kept the site undeveloped, but wells and cisterns finally made the new capital habitable. Unfortunately, centuries later, Herod the Great's builders put down foundations so deep that only scraps of Old Testament Samaria escaped destruction.

In 876 B.C., the Assyrian king Assurnasirpal marched his army west to the Mediterranean, inflicting heavy damage en route. The Assyrians covered their walls with reliefs of vanquished cities and enemies, and texts detailed the ways that people were treated when they did not surrender:

> I built a pillar against his city gate, and I flayed all the chief men . . . and I covered the pillar with their skins . . . some I impaled upon the pillar on stakes . . . and I cut off the limbs of the officers . . . many captives from among them I burned with fire . . . from some I cut off their hands and from others I cut off their noses, their ears, and their fingers, of many I put out the eyes . . . . (Roux 290–91)

In this campaign Assurnasirpal became aware that there was a 'land of Omri' south of Syria. The future destroyer of Israel had come on stage.

David had conquered Moab, but Moab broke free at Solomon's death. The next biblical reference to Moab is in 2 Kings 3:4 where it is mentioned that Ahab received tribute from the Moabites. Nowhere does the Bible say who brought Moab back into line. But the Moabite Stone does – it was Omri. That Omri reclaimed Moab is relatively unimportant, but it is something that had puzzled scholars until the Moabite Stone supplied the answer.

Ahab repeatedly fought the Syrians, but in 853 B.C. he joined with them and other kings to fight the Assyrians, who were coming west again, this time led by Shalmaneser III. The two sides met at Karkar in northern Syria. If one believes the Assyrian rhetoric, Shalmaneser III won a glorious victory:

> I spread their corpses everywhere, filling the entire plain with their widely scattered fleeing soldiers. During the battle I made their blood flow . . . with their corpses I spanned the Orontes before there was a bridge. (*ANET* 279)

The battle of Karkar represents the first physical contact between Israel and Assyria. Scholars are inclined to believe that, if the Assyrians did indeed win, it was at a great cost. For the next several years, the Assyrians were not able to mount another strong offensive westwards. Nothing is said about the battle of Karkar in the Bible because the biblical writers were interested in Ahab's religious, not his military, activities. But from the Assyrian account, it can be concluded that Ahab was one of the more powerful kings of the mid-ninth century B.C. In the coalition that confronted the Assyrians, only the Syrians had a larger army than Israel, and Ahab fielded more than half the chariots. (Some archaeologists – see page 18 – date the 'stables' found at Megiddo to Ahab.)

Late Divided Kingdom 841–722 B.C.

During the Early Divided Kingdom, the relations between Judah and Israel went from war-like to warming to close co-operation. However, in 841 B.C., that friendship was permanently broken when Jehu killed the kings of both Judah and Israel and seized the throne of Israel.

Assyria and Israel

That same year Shalmaneser III again led his Assyrian army westward. This time, there was no coalition to confront him as had gathered at Karkar twelve years earlier. Hazael of Damascus lost thousands of troops in this renewed conflict, his city survived a siege, but its surrounding landscape was devastated. Jehu was among those who survived by paying tribute:

> The tribute of Jehu . . . I received from him silver, gold, a golden saplu-bowl, a golden vase with pointed bottom, golden tumblers, golden buckets, tin, a staff for a king and a wooden puruhtu. (*ANET* 281)

This payment is not recorded in the Bible, but is found on the Black Obelisk of Shalmaneser, which commemorates several years of that king's military campaigns. From the obelisk we learn that during the reign of Jehu, Israel paid its first tribute to the Assyrians.

The Assyrians repeatedly harassed Israel, but there is one instance where their actions seem to have been of help. The Bible characterizes Jehoahaz (Jehu's son) as an evil king, but it also tells us that he called on the Lord when he was hard pressed by Syria. Then there is the cryptic note in 2 Kings 13:4–5 that God 'listened to' Jehoahaz and gave him a 'deliverer'. This deliverer is not named in the Bible, but was probably the Assyrian king Adad-nirari III, who invaded Syria about 803 B.C., forcing Syria to pull back to protect its own lands – and thus saving Israel.

Peace and Prosperity

During the reign of Jeroboam II, Israel was able to extend its borders to where they had been in the time of David and Solomon (2 Kings 14:25, 28). The Bible does not relate the details of how Jeroboam managed this expansion, but political conditions were certainly right: Syria was still weak from earlier Assyrian attacks, and Assyria was preoccupied with Armenia.

Broken pieces of jars and bowls were sometimes used as notepads (see page 27), and several dozen such sherds dating to the reign of Jeroboam II have been found at Samaria. These *'ostraca'* served as temporary records of commodities being delivered into the capital city, and they contain the names of people, officials and settlements not mentioned in the Bible. Individually they are of little importance (one reads, for example: 'In the tenth year. From Hazeroth to Gaddiyau. A jar of fine oil.'), but collectively they reveal the prosperity and dense agricultural population that existed in the region of Samaria.

The Bible records that under Uzziah, Judah also became prosperous. Here too archaeology provides insights. Pharaoh Shishak's raid (see p. 20) had destroyed forts and settlements in the south of the country. Archaeological surveys found the same area experienced a building boom during Uzziah's reign.

Decline

When Tiglath-pileser III ascended the throne of Assyria he began to form an empire greater than anything the Near East had ever seen. Meanwhile, Jeroboam II of Israel had a long and successful reign. He died peacefully, but his son died violently as Israel entered a period of confusion culminating in its collapse and extinction. Israel's decline began in 743 B.C., when the Assyrian army marched west to the Mediterranean. Tiglath-pileser III received homage and tribute along the way:

> I received tribute from . . . Rezon of Damascus, Menahem of Samaria, Hiram of Tyre . . . to wit gold, silver, tin, iron, elephant hides . . . whatever was precious enough for a royal treasure . . . also lambs whose stretched hides were dyed purple, and wild birds whose spread-out

One panel from the Black Obelisk of Shalmaneser III. It depicts Jehu kneeling before the Assyrian king. Attendants flank the two men.

wings were dyed blue, furthermore horses, mules, large and small cattle . . . As for Menahem I overwhelmed him like a snowstorm and he . . . bowed to my feet. . . . (*ANET* 283–84)

The Bible says Menahem exacted 50 shekels of silver from each wealthy man in order to raise sufficient tribute (2 Kings 15:19–20). Assyrian records show that 50 shekels was then the standard price for a slave. Therefore, to remain free, the wealthy had to pay the equivalent of their slave price.

A few years later, Israel and Syria made the fatal mistake of believing that they could stand up to the Assyrians. When King Ahaz of Judah was pressed to join them, he sent tribute to Tiglath-pileser III and begged for help (2 Kings 16:7). In response, in 733 B.C., Tiglath-pileser III crushed Syria and turned the northern half of Israel into an Assyrian province.

At this point, the Bible first mentions deportation. Tiglath-pileser III introduced the policy of deporting captives rather than killing them. By keeping them alive, the Assyrians could continue to extract tribute. And by moving people far away from their homeland it was hoped the likelihood of their revolting would be diminished. This policy was especially effective with

Relief of Tiglath-pileser III of Assyria in his chariot. Here the king is accompanied by one man holding the reins and another who holds the umbrella shading the king.

people who believed that their gods were limited to a particular geographical area.

The Fall of Israel

Widespread revolt followed the death of Tiglath-pileser III. Hoshea, then king of Israel, joined the revolt, but was forced back into line by the new Assyrian king, Shalmaneser V. When Hoshea revolted a second time, the city of Samaria came under siege. Three years later, in 722 B.C., the city fell to Sargon II:

I besieged and conquered Samaria, led away as booty 27,290 inhabitants of it. I formed from among them a contingent of 50 chariots and made [the] remaining inhabitants assume their social positions. I installed over them an officer of mine and imposed upon them the tribute of the former king. (*ANET* 284–5)

With the fall of Samaria, Israel ceased to exist, and the border of the Assyrian empire was extended to within about 48 kilometres (30 miles) of Jerusalem.

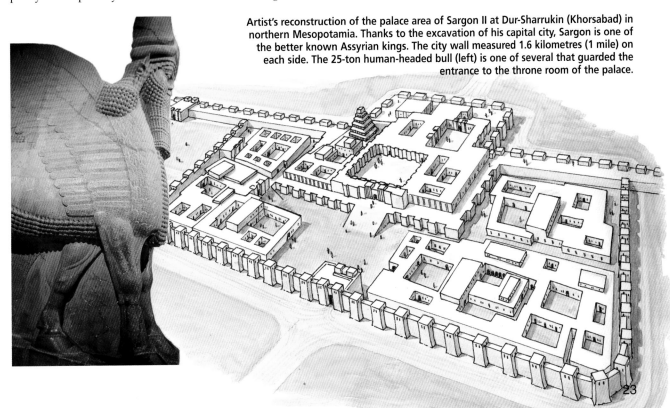

Artist's reconstruction of the palace area of Sargon II at Dur-Sharrukin (Khorsabad) in northern Mesopotamia. Thanks to the excavation of his capital city, Sargon is one of the better known Assyrian kings. The city wall measured 1.6 kilometres (1 mile) on each side. The 25-ton human-headed bull (left) is one of several that guarded the entrance to the throne room of the palace.

Judah Alone I
Hezekiah (716–687 B.C.)

Above: One of two known copies of the 'Sennacherib Prism'. Both are six-sided, made of baked clay, and record Sennacherib's military campaigns, including his incursions into Judah.
Below: The Siloam Inscription. This was damaged late in the nineteenth century, when thieves clumsily cut it from the tunnel wall. Fortunately casts of the inscription had been made before this happened.

Hezekiah and Sargon II

Hezekiah took the throne of Judah six years after Israel's fall. Four or five years later there were stirrings of unrest within the Assyrian empire. According to the Assyrians:

> Philistia, Judah, Edom, Moab . . . payers of tribute and tax . . . [contacted the] king of Egypt, a prince who could not save them, they sent their presents and attempted to gain him as an ally. (*ANET* 287)

This uprising was quickly put down; Isaiah 20:1 mentions the capture of Ashdod. According to the quotation above, Hezekiah had been paying tribute to maintain Judah's freedom.

Hezekiah and Sennacherib

Rebellion broke out in 705 B.C. when Sargon II died. Only three neighbouring kings remained loyal to Assyria, and Hezekiah put one of them in prison. We learn of this development from Sennacherib, Sargon II's son and successor:

> The officials, the patricians and the common people of Ekron – who had thrown Padi, their king, into fetters because he was loyal to his solemn oath sworn [to my god], and had handed him over to Hezekiah, the Jew – and Hezekiah held him in pris-

on, unlawfully, as if Padi were an enemy. (*ANET* 287)

Hezekiah knew that the Assyrians would respond, and he began to prepare his country for war. In Jerusalem the Gihon spring, on its eastern slope, was redirected into a new pool – the Pool of Siloam – at the south end of the city.

Of all his preparations, 'Hezekiah's tunnel' is the most famous. This tunnel meanders some 532 metres (1,750 feet) through limestone bedrock, and at places it is 30 metres (100 or more feet) below the surface. Recent studies suggest the tunnel's circuitous route from the spring to the pool follows natural fractures in the bedrock. Although indirect, this route was easier to dig.

When the tunnel was completed, an inscription (the 'Siloam Inscription') was cut into a side wall just inside the south entrance. Although damaged, the preserved part of this inscription still gives an insight into how the work was done:

> . . . And this was the way in which it was cut through: While . . . were still . . . axes, each man toward his fellow, and while there were still three cubits to be cut through, there was heard the voice of a man calling to his fellow, for there was an overlap in the rock on the right and on the left. [*One crew started at the spring, and another at the pool.*] And when the tunnel was driven through, the quarrymen hewed the rock, each man toward his fellow, axe against axe; and the water flowed from the spring toward the reservoir. . . . (*ANET* 321)

Gravity feeds the water from the spring into the pool, where people went to fill their water jars. Today, tourists wade through the tunnel to get a sense of the back-breaking labour that went into the project.

Sennacherib Invades

Sennacherib had some initial distractions at home, but in 701 B.C. he finally led his army into Judah. Dozens of cities were destroyed. Excavations at several Judean sites have found hundreds of jar handles stamped *'lmlk* – 'belonging to the king'. The handles are from storage jars which held provisions stockpiled in anticipation of Assyrian attack. At more than one of these sites the handles were found in destruction levels dating to Hezekiah's reign.

> I assaulted Ekron and killed the officials and patricians who had committed the crime and hung their bodies on poles surrounding the city. The common citizens who were guilty of minor crimes, I considered prisoners of war . . . I made Padi, their king, come from Jerusalem and set him as their lord on the throne. . . . As to Hezekiah, the Jew, he did not submit to my yoke. I laid siege to forty-six of his strong cities, walled forts and the countless small villages in their vicinity and conquered them by means of well-stamped earth-ramps and battering rams brought near to the walls. . . . I drove out of them 200,150 people, young and old, male and female, horses, mules, donkeys, big and small cattle beyond counting. . . . (*ANET* 288)

Sennacherib was especially proud of his conquest of Lachish, and in his palace at Nineveh nearly 21 metres (70 linear feet) of wall reliefs were devoted to the fall of that city. The excavations at Lachish add their own details. The ramps which the Assyrians built in order to bring their siege towers up against the city wall have been found. The excavations also uncovered hundreds of arrowheads that had been spewed into the city. Even more graphic was the discovery of a mass grave into which over 1,500 bodies had been dumped after the city's fall.

> [Hezekiah] I made a prisoner in Jerusalem, his royal residence, like a bird in a cage. . . . His towns that I had plundered I took away from his country and gave them to [other kings]. . . . (*ANET* 288)

One scene from the 'Lachish Reliefs' found in the palace of Sennacherib. It shows the ramps thrown against the outer of two defensive walls and the leather-clad siege towers which were wheeled up them to dismantle the wall. Men pour water over the towers to prevent fire arrows from igniting them. Archers, some firing from behind large wicker shields, shoot arrows into the city. The scene is composite in time: it shows both the heat of battle and its aftermath, as Judeans file out through the city gate into captivity. Three Judeans are seen impaled on stakes near the city gate.

The biblical record says Hezekiah and Judah paid dearly. The words of Sennacherib's Prism, the reliefs on his palace walls and the archaeological discoveries at Lachish and elsewhere make it clear just how dearly.

Hezekiah and Merodach-baladin

Shortly afterwards, Hezekiah was approached by envoys from Merodach-baladin (Isaiah 39). For years Merodach-baladin had been declaring himself king of Babylon and trying to break free of Assyrian control. The Assyrians would put him to flight, only to find him back again. His envoys were probably hoping to find in Hezekiah an ally against Assyria. Fortunately, nothing came of this contact because Merodach-baladin was soon sent fleeing for one last time. By contrast, Hezekiah's last years seem to have been prosperous. Settlement increased in the Negev, and Jerusalem

A boundary stone depicting Merodach-baladin, on the left, conferring a land grant to an official.

grew to the largest size it would reach in Old Testament times.

Judah Alone II
Manasseh–Zedekiah (686–586 B.C.)

Stele of Esarhaddon. The Assyrian king is shown holding ropes attached to rings through the lips (?) of two of his enemies. The stele illustrates the action (the 'hook' in 2 Chronicles 33:11) taken against Manasseh.

Manasseh

Perhaps Manasseh's greatest accomplishment as king was to keep Judah free from total Assyrian control. He did this in part by paying tribute. In the reign of Esarhaddon, son of Sennacherib, Manasseh is listed among twenty-two kings who were made to:

> transport under terrible difficulties, to Nineveh, the town where I exercise my [Esarhaddon's] rulership . . . building material for my palace: big logs, long beams and thin boards from cedar and pine trees, products of the Sirara and Lebanon mountains, which had grown for a long time into tall and strong timber, also from their quarries. (*ANET* 291)

In 671 B.C. Esarhaddon invaded Egypt and made it another province within his empire. Assyria had never seemed so strong, but less than twenty years later there came a first sign of weakness; Egypt declared its independence. It was probably to keep Judah from entertaining similar thoughts that Ashurbanipal 'put a hook in [Manasseh's] nose, bound him with bronze shackles and took him to Babylon' (2 Chronicles 33:11).

Josiah

The Bible concentrates on Josiah's reforms and makes no mention of the political scene during the first half of his reign. But it was in those years that the Assyrian empire suddenly began to collapse. In 626 B.C., Scythians and Cimmerians swept south out of Armenia, and Assyria lost all territories west of the Euphrates river. That same year a Chaldean named Nabopolassar captured Babylon and declared southern Mesopotamia free. Thanks to these events, Judah no longer had to send tribute to the Assyrians. The prophet Nahum vividly predicted the fall of the Assyrian capital city, Nineveh, but did not identify the destroyers. A Chaldean chronicle does. It tells how, in 612 B.C., the Chaldeans and the Medes joined forces and:

Relief from the palace of Ashurbanipal at Nineveh. Some walls in his palace were covered with scenes of battle, and others with hunting in his game preserve. In this more peaceful scene, Ashurbanipal and his queen relax in a garden. They are accompanied by fan-bearers, a servant bringing food and another servant playing a lyre. But on the left, the head of King Teuman of Elam hangs from a tree.

Lachish Letter 2. In this time of impending doom the ostracon opens with customary words of hope: 'May God cause my lord to hear tidings of peace this very day, this very day!'

A *bulla* (plural *bullae*) is a lump of clay that was placed over string used to tie a papyrus document closed. The clay was then impressed with a seal and, when the clay dried, the document could not be tampered with without discovery. *Bullae* are generally only thumbnail in size. The one enlarged here reads, 'Belonging to Berekhyahu son of Neriyahu the scribe'. This is the Baruch of Jeremiah 36:4. On the seal his name carries the suffix abbreviation for God (-*yahu*), indicating that his full name was 'blessed of God'. Neriah in Jeremiah 36 and 'Neriyahu' on the seal are the same individual. Baruch's *bulla* may even retain his fingerprint impression.

> pitched camp against Nineveh . . . Three battles were fought, then they made a great attack against the city . . . the city was seized and a great defeat [was] inflicted upon the entire population. On that day . . . many prisoners of the city, beyond counting, they carried away. The city they turned into ruin-hills and heaps of debris. (*ANET* 304–05)

The fall of Assyria reawakened the Egyptian dream of empire and their army began to move northwards. In 609 B.C., Josiah was mortally wounded in a battle at Megiddo.

Puppet Kings

Three months after Josiah's death, the Egyptians carried off in chains his son, Jehoahaz, and installed another son, Jehoiakim, as their puppet on the Judean throne. Jeremiah levelled such strong criticisms at Jehoiakim (see Jeremiah 22) that the prophet was forced into hiding and communicated through his scribe, Baruch. In 1975 a *bulla* containing Baruch's name was found, suggesting that he had been a royal scribe before making a career change to work for Jeremiah.

Egypt's hope of a revived empire ended in 605 B.C. when its army was crushed by the Chaldeans at Carchemish in northern Syria (see Jeremiah 46). When King Nebuchadnezzar swept south, Jehoiakim became a puppet king of the Chaldeans. Tribute and Judean exiles flowed eastwards. A few years later Jehoiakim unwisely withheld tribute. He was perhaps fortunate to have died before the Chaldean army reached Jerusalem. Their chronicles read that in Nebuchadnezzar's seventh year the latter:

> called up his army, marched against Syria, encamped against the city of Judah and seized the town on the second day of the month Adar. He captured the king. He appointed there a [governor] of his own choice. He took much booty from it and sent it to Babylon. (*ANET* 564)

Jehoiakim's son, Jehoiachin, had hardly warmed the throne before he was captured and carried off into Chaldean exile. Zedekiah, the youngest son of Josiah, was the puppet installed by Nebuchadnezzar. In time, Zedekiah also withheld tribute. Predictably, this brought Nebuchadnezzar back into Judah and the rebuilt city of Lachish came under attack.

The Lachish Letters

Twenty-one *ostraca* were found during the excavation of a room in the city gate at Lachish. Known as the 'Lachish Letters', these documents contain some of the last records of Judah. In Jeremiah 34:7 only the major cities of Lachish, Azekah and Jerusalem were still standing. One *ostracon* mentions a fire-signal system by which cities communicated. Either the writer was not in a position to see Azekah when he wrote, or the city had by then been captured:

> And let my lord know that we are watching for the signals of Lachish, according to all the indications that my lord has given, for we cannot see Azekah. (*ANET* 322)

In Jeremiah 38:4 there is a request that Jeremiah be put to death because he was lowering morale. A similar charge is levelled in one of the Lachish Letters:

> And behold the words of the pr[ ] are not good, but to weaken our hands. . . . (*ANET* 322)

The key word is incomplete; in the original published edition of the Lachish Letters, it was suggested that the reference is to Jeremiah. In 586 B.C. Jerusalem went up in flames.

The Exile

The Nature of the Exile

Thousands of Jews had been taken east into exile, first by the Assyrians and then by the Chaldeans. However, not everyone went into exile, and not everyone who did suffered excessively. The Bible makes it clear that families were not torn apart, and it seems that a form of local self-government was allowed in exile. It is also clear that when people returned home some had become wealthy.

Archaeological evidence suggests that many exiles chose not to go home when it became possible. More than seven hundred business documents found in the city of Nippur, south-east of Babylon, contain several dozen Jewish names. These documents date to the end of the fifth century B.C., well after the exile.

A disinclination to return home can also be found in correspondence between Jews living at Elephantine, on Egypt's southern border, and Jews in Judea. The Jews in Egypt had specific problems and needs, but none of their letters suggest any hint of a desire to return home.

Nebuchadnezzar

Of the thousands of Jews who were taken into exile, Ezekiel and Daniel are among the most prominent. Ezekiel became a prophet to those in exile while, initially, Daniel was selected for training as a scribe. There were many different linguistic groups within the Chaldean empire, and it was necessary to have scribes to translate official edicts into whichever local languages were relevant before they were sent out

The Ishtar Gate as reconstructed at the site.

into the empire. Likewise, when communications in a local language arrived, a scribe was needed to translate the document for the Chaldeans.

Dream interpretation was still extremely important, and catalogues in which hundreds of dreams and interpretations have been collected have been found. When Nebuchadnezzar had a dream (Daniel 2) his men would have searched through explanatory lists like the following:

> If he eats meat
>   he knows peace of mind.
> If he eats the flesh of his friend
>   he will enjoy a large share.
> If his friend eats his face
>   he will enjoy a large share.
> If he eats the flesh of his hand
>   his daughter will die.
> If he eats the flesh of his foot
>   his eldest son will die.
> (Oppenheim 279)

Daniel's three friends were thrown into a 'blazing furnace' (Daniel 3). Almost certainly, this was one of the many large brick kilns used to fire face bricks to make important structures more durable. Jeremiah 29:22 records an earlier instance, when Nebuchadnezzar had two men burned to death in this way. There are also extra-biblical references to this practice.

The city of Babylon, based on the excavations undertaken.

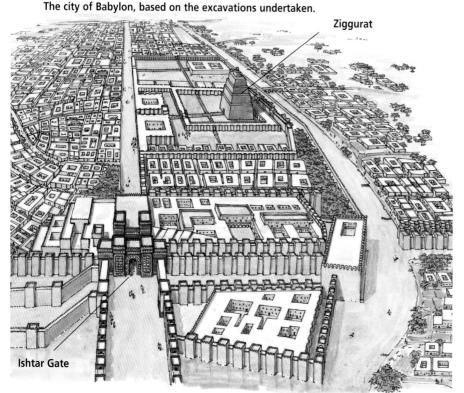

Ziggurat

Ishtar Gate

Babylon

Daniel would have been familiar with Babylon. Its inner city covered some 202 hectares (500 acres) and was protected by three walls and a moat. The whole city spread over some 1,214 hectares (3,000 acres) and was protected by an outer wall more than 21 metres (70 feet) wide, broad enough for chariots to pass each other as they drove along the top of the ramparts. Nine gates gave access to the inner city. Of these, the Ishtar Gate, which sat close to the palace, is the best known. The location of the 'hanging gardens of Babylon', one of the 'seven wonders of the ancient world' is uncertain. Nebuchadnezzar was extremely proud of Babylon:

> A great wall which like a mountain cannot be moved I made of mortar and brick. . . . Its foundation upon the bosom of the abyss . . . its top I raised mountain high. I triplicated the city wall in order to strengthen it, I caused a great protecting wall to run at the foot of the wall of burnt brick. . . . A third great moat-wall . . . I built with mortar and brick. . . . The palace . . . I rebuilt in Babylon with great cedars I brought from Lebanon, the beautiful forest to roof it. . . . Huge cedars from Lebanon . . . with radiant gold I over-laid them, with jewels I adorned them. (Thompson 191–93)

The Chaldean dynasty was founded by Nebuchadnezzar's father. Under Nebuchadnezzar, the Chaldeans reached their peak in wealth and power, but less than twenty-five years after his death, in 562 B.C., the Chaldean empire had been swept

away. Nebuchadnezzar was succeeded by his son Evil-Merodach. (The first part of his name is not a description of his personality; it can also be transliterated 'Awil'.) In his first year, Evil-Merodach released Jehoiachin from house arrest and provided him with a regular allowance (2 Kings 25:27–30). Despite the astronomical odds against finding evidence of such a provision, a cuneiform tablet found at Babylon says that:

> For Jehoiachin king of the land of Judah, for the five sons of the king of the land of Judah, and for eight Judeans, each one half sila of grain. . . . (Saggs 132)

Evil-Merodach was assassinated after having ruled for only two years. A power struggle followed, after which Nabonidus became king. He apparently had more interest in worshipping the moon god than in honouring the national god, Marduk. This preference was not popular with his subjects.

For some unexplained reason, Nabonidus vacated Babylon and moved to Tema, deep in the Arabian desert. The Babylonian Chronicle reports that Nabonidus then appointed his son Belshazzar as co-regent in Babylon. Nabonidus prayed:

> O Moon god preserve me, Nabonidus, king of Babylon. . . . To me give the gift of long life, and as regards Belshazzar, my first-born son, my dear offspring, put in his heart reverence for thy high divinity. (Thomas 90)

The fragmented tablet that contains reference to Jehoiachin and his sons.

A few years earlier Nabonidus had made the mistake of encouraging Cyrus the Persian against the Medes. Cyrus not only took control of the Medes, but began chipping away at the Chaldean empire itself. By 539 B.C., Babylon came under siege. Knowing the defences of the city, we can understand how Belshazzar might have thought himself safe enough to hold the famous banquet during which Daniel interpreted the handwriting on the palace wall (Daniel 5); but Babylon fell only hours later as Persian forces moved into the city. Only the citadel offered resistance. Belshazzar died, Nabonidus was captured but treated kindly. The Persian empire had begun:

> [Marduk the god of Babylon] beheld with pleasure Cyrus's good deeds and his upright mind and therefore ordered him to march against his city Babylon. He made him set out on the road to Babylon, going at his side like a real friend. His widespread troops . . . strolled along, their weapons packed away. Without any battle, he made him enter his town Babylon, sparing Babylon any calamity. . . . All the inhabitants of Babylon as well as of the entire country . . . bowed to Cyrus and kissed his feet, jubilant that he had received the kingship. . . . (*ANET* 315–16)

The Cyrus Cylinder, which records that king's capture of Babylon.

The Restoration

that famous conflict the Persians are said to have lost 6,400 men to only 192 Greeks. This last figure has the ring of authenticity, since each of the Greek dead is recorded by name. Darius died in 485 B.C.

Cyrus the Great

As Persian power grew, Cyrus took a new approach to empire building. Instead of ruling by fear and deportation, Cyrus tried to make people content to be part of his empire – even allowing them to return to their ancestral homes if they so chose.

50,000 Jews returned to Palestine, which is a small number compared with the more than 200,000 people said to have been deported during the reign of Hezekiah alone. Initially the returnees were pressed into a small strip of hill country centred around Jerusalem, but in time they were able to expand these boundaries. Archaeologists have evidence of this expansion in seal impressions marked Yehud (Judah) from storage jars found at a number of surrounding sites.

Cyrus died in 530 B.C., in a meaningless skirmish against some eastern tribes. His son, Cambyses, left a short shadow on history and the Bible ignores him completely.

Darius the Great

Darius the Great became king of Persia in 522 B.C. Two years later he received a letter from the governor of the district of Samaria. Work was progressing on the Jewish temple in Jerusalem, and the governor was inquiring whether Cyrus had given the project official sanction. The Persian archives were searched and a favourable response was sent back to Samaria.

A careful reading of the book of Haggai shows that the waiting time for this reply was less than four months, and archaeology suggests the response could have arrived much sooner than that. The Persians put a high priority on communication, and a Royal Road stretched some 2,700 kilometres (1,700 miles) from Susa to Sardis, near the western shores of Anatolia (modern Turkey). This road was dotted with post stations and fresh mounts for the couriers. A letter written in Susa could reach Sardis in one week. Even lacking time estimates for the secondary routes, a month should have been adequate to check the archives and get a response back to Samaria. The fifth-century Greek historian Herodotus was so impressed with the Persian mail system that he wrote:

> Neither snow, nor rain, nor heat, nor gloom of night stays these couriers from the swift completion of their appointed rounds. (*Herodotus* 8.98)

Darius blamed the mainland Greeks for repeated unrest in Ionia, western Anatolia, which he claimed for Persia. Battles were fought with some success for the Persians – until the battle of Marathon in 490 B.C. In

Xerxes and Esther

Xerxes (Ahasuerus in the book of Esther) was the son of Darius. The Bible does not explain why he held the banquet mentioned in the opening chapter of Esther. One suggestion is that the festivity was part of the preparations for a campaign to pay back the Greeks for his father's defeat at Marathon.

Xerxes took to Greece a large army – its exact size is debated – and met little resistance until he was stopped temporarily at the narrow pass of Thermopylae. The willingness of a few hundred Spartans to die defending the pass bought Athens more time to evacuate, and is celebrated in Greek history. Athens fell and the Acropolis was burned. Then Xerxes suffered the humiliation of watching his fleet being defeated by the Greeks in the bay of Salamis. The Persian land army probably could have overrun the rest of Greece, but Xerxes had had enough. He withdrew and returned home.

The tomb of Cyrus. Persian religion forbade burial in the ground. The tomb stands about 10.5 metres (35 feet) above the garden that once surrounded it.

This treasury scene at Persepolis depicts a seated Darius receiving a report from one of his commanders. Xerxes, then crown prince, stands behind his father on the dais.

The Greek campaign lasted approximately three years and was prior to the beauty contest of Esther chapter 2. Xerxes spent the rest of his life moving from one to another of his capitals, amusing himself with building projects and women. These years were also filled with court intrigue. The plot against Xerxes recorded in Esther 2:21–23 was not an isolated event, and an assassination attempt finally succeeded in 465 B.C.

Artaxerxes I, Ezra and Nehemiah

Artaxerxes was not in line for the throne, but murdered his older brother to become king. In his seventh year, 457 B.C., Artaxerxes commissioned Ezra to oversee both religious and political affairs in Judah (Ezra 7–10). Persia had earlier conquered Egypt, but Egypt had rebelled. The Persians wanted to

ensure that their land bridge into Egypt remained secure. In 454 B.C. the Persian army marched westward and regained control of Egypt. Ezra had kept the peace.

In the twentieth year of Artaxerxes, the Persian king allowed Nehemiah to go to Jerusalem and rebuild its city walls. Despite opposition, in fifty-two days the work was accomplished. Nehemiah chapter 3 and archaeological studies show that the city wall was not so much built as repaired. The workers were largely filling breaks in the wall and putting up gates in a Jerusalem slightly smaller than in Solomon's day.

As a final archaeological note to the Old Testament: coins are first mentioned in the Bible in the books of Ezra and Nehemiah. The first use of coins is credited to King Croesus of Sardis, in the middle of the sixth century B.C. The Persians learned of the innovation when their armies marched across Anatolia, and the practice spread within the empire.

Looking down on Persepolis, one of the five Persian capitals. Although the story of Esther is set in Susa, the treasury city of Persepolis is best able to provide a sense of the world that Esther would have known. A is the palace area, B the Apadana (audience room) where the columns still standing are each nearly 21 metres (70 feet) tall. The treasury building of Darius is C, and of Xerxes D. Much of the construction, now gone, was in mud-brick, which cooled the interiors.

Index

Copyright © 2008 Lion Hudson plc/ Tim Dowley Associates

Published in 2010 by Kregel Publications, a division of Kregel, Inc., P.O. Box 2607, Grand Rapids, Michigan, 49501.

Worldwide co-edition produced by:
Lion Hudson plc
Wilkinson House,
Jordan Hill Road
Oxford OX2 8DR England
Tel: +44 (0) 1865 302750
Fax: +44 (0) 1865 302757
Email: coed@lionhudson.com
www.lionhudson.com

ISBN: 978-0-8254-2740-4

Printed in China